Presented to

_____

From

_____

Date

_____

DEAREST MOTHER,
Dearest Friend

INSPIRATION FROM THE JOURNALS AND LETTERS
OF CATHERINE MARSHALL

CATHERINE MARSHALL

J. Countryman, Nashville TN

Copyright © 2001 by Marshall-LeSourd L.L.C.
All rights reserved throughout the world.

Published by J. Countryman, a division of Thomas Nelson, Inc.,
Nashville, Tennessee 37214.

Compiled and edited by Terri Gibbs

Produced in association with the brand development agency
of Evergreen Ideas, Inc. on behalf of Marshall-LeSourd L. L. C.
For more information on Catherine Marshall,
visit www.CatherineMarshall.com

Designed by Uttley / DouPonce DesignWorks,
Sisters, Oregon

ISBN: 08499-5767-2
www.jcountryman.com

Printed and bound in Belgium

"May the Lord bless and keep

you . . . till we meet over there

in the glory of His amazin' love.

And I'm that beholden to you

for bringin' yer brightness to

take away some of an old lady's

lonesomeness. Thank ye, lassie."

—AUNT POLLY
in *Christy*

Leonora Wood and her daughter
Sarah Catherine

September 1, 1972

Lord, I especially want to thank you this
morning for my mother. How blessed I am
to have had you choose such a woman to bear me!
I thank you for her lifelong gentleness . . .
her womanliness . . . her unwavering faithfulness . . .
the vision that always could lift her hopes and
dreams on wings and send them flying above
and beyond drudgery or mundane circumstances.
Always she has been a true mother to all
children and grandchildren.

Lord, thank You. I love her.
Bless her bountifully this day.

Catherine

ith over thirty million books sold, Catherine
Marshall is one of America's most notable and best-
selling Christian writers. She is also one of America's most
beloved authors. Catherine wrote with candor, simplicity, and
eloquence about the deepest issues of the human heart. Her
more than twenty books have all been classics in the field of
inspirational writing. Two of them, *A Man Called Peter* and
Christy, also became hugely successful movies.

Throughout her life, and always with the comfort and
inspiration of God's Word, Catherine sought to meet head-on
the difficult questions of life. Questions about obedience, self-
surrender, doubt, and prayer. Her deep probing and the answers
she discovered were incorporated into her writing. One has only
to read a few pages of any one of her books to know that her pen
was truly guided by a prayer-filled heart.

But Catherine Marshall the writer can never be separated from Catherine Marshall LeSourd, the family woman. All her best-selling books have had their roots in the spiritual interplay of husband and wife, parent and child, elderly parents, and family friends. Her success as a writer has always been rooted in her willingness to share her deepest heartaches. This readiness to be vulnerable has touched and helped literally millions of readers.

The material in this book, which emphasizes the loving and interdependent relationship between Catherine and her mother, covers the span of Catherine's life from girlhood as a Presbyterian pastor's daughter to her college years in Georgia. From her experiences as the wife of Peter Marshall, chaplain of the Senate, to early widowhood, single parenting, remarriage, and raising a second family. The selections are drawn from articles, daily journals, and the personal letters of both Catherine and her mother, Leonora Wood—a gentle, indomitable woman who was the original heroine of Catherine's best-selling novel, *Christy*.

Leonora was a cheerful woman, a minister's wife with a people-rooted ministry all her own. At nineteen, almost half a century before the Peace Corps, she taught and worked with the impoverished people of Morgan Gap— a Smokey Mountain community forgotten by the rest of the world. During the Depression of the thirties, with ingenuity and thrift, she fed and clothed not only her own family but the needy of the community as well. When the town of Keyser was caught in paralysis, she waged a one-woman campaign to seek help for the destitute, going out alone to the slum section of Radical Hill, where she visited shack after filthy shack, organized an afternoon Sunday school, and taught basic homemaking skills.

When reminiscing about her childhood in West Virginia, Catherine's conversation always turned to her mother. A knock on the front door of their home was invariably answered with a shout from the depths of the house, "Come on back to the kitchen!" And there at the kitchen table in a disarray of children would be her mother—tall, gentle, blue-eyed, and fragile, but with what Catherine called "a great tensile strength." Whether in the kitchen making biscuits, on the porch shelling peas, or in the fields seeking wildflowers, her great passion was to relate stories of history (one of her consuming interests) and to share God's love from the great depths of her Christian faith.

Mrs. Wood's influence on Catherine's life was profound. She was the single most important person in shaping her daughter's life, and the two enjoyed a remarkably close friendship throughout their lives. If faith can be inherited, Catherine's was inherited from her mother. If qualities of living—a sense of day-to-day adventure and a willingness to work hard to achieve a goal—can be passed along to another, Catherine owes these, too, to her mother.

I hope you will enjoy this rare glimpse into the private, loving, and extraordinary lives of these two unforgettable Christian women—Catherine Marshall LeSourd and her beloved mother, Leonora Wood.

TERRI GIBBS
Editor

God insists on seeing us one by one, each a special case, each inestimably beloved for Himself.

–CRISTY HUDDLESTON
in *Christy*

Sarah Catherine Wood

y oldest memory, still one of the brightest of all the wonderful experiences I have known, is of my mother taking my baby hand and leading me to a bed of spring hyacinths in the side yard of the old manse where we lived in Canton, Mississippi. There she showed me the perfect bell-shaped flowerettes packed on their stiff stems—cream and blue and lavender and pink. I remember burying my face in their delicious fragrance.

A tiny episode? Perhaps. But because of my mother, it remains to this day one of my lifetime's shimmering moments. . . . It was a way of looking at life that was forever to influence me. "No one," as mother put it for me in words when I was older, "is ever poor so long as he can see and cherish any part of God's lovely creation." That thought, so lovely in itself, has buoyed me countless times when my spirit felt poor indeed.

In my childhood there were times, of course, when it seemed as if Dad's small pastor's salary made us poor. (How typical it was that when he died that May day in 1961, his checking account balance was exactly sixty-eight cents.) Yet there was the natural abundance around us that Mother taught us to appreciate.

Day by day she showed me that the thick green carpet of moss under the towering oaks was really a child's playroom. That the sandbox could provide castles so carefully and imaginatively constructed as to be worthy of princes and princesses. That the sweet peas climbing up their string trellises were actually fine ladies in pastel-hued frocks. Even the battered old coal-house became an enchanting forest cottage as the wisteria smothered it in green and lavender.

With such wondrous vision, Mother taught me that out beyond the bed of hyacinths, the sand castles and the oak trees— farther than I could see even when pumping high in my swing— was a world bursting with beauty and adventure. Her blue-gray eyes would light up as she told me, "The sky is the limit, Catherine. What you can achieve some day is restricted only by how far you can stretch your horizons, by your capacity for appreciation, and by your faith in God's willingness to help."

MOTHER BELIEVED IN ACTION

Mother was sitting on top of a rock in the middle of Morgan's Branch, the day Father first saw her. He thought she looked rather like a penguin—blue serge skirt, white shirt-waist—only penguins don't ordinarily have blue eyes and sit in the middle of frozen creeks reading books. Somehow Father never forgot the date. It was December 29, 1909. A gigantic snowstorm had covered all of east Tennessee just three days earlier, so it wasn't exactly rock-sitting weather.

Mother had come to teach at the Ebenezer Mission school in the Great Smokey Mountains of East Tennessee. She had gotten off the train at the Del Rio station in the middle of the storm, only to discover that no transportation was available to the Mission. Snow drifts had made the crude trails through Pigeon Roost Gap, across the half-frozen Gillot Branch, and up and down the ravines of Chestnut Ridge all but impassable. . . . So Mother—feeling some-what frustrated in her first missionary journey—spent the night near the Del Rio station at Mrs. Burnett's boarding house.

The Ezenezer Mission was founded in 1908 by Dr. Edward O. Guerrant, a Kentucky physician. During the War Between the States, the little Frenchman, en route to Virginia to join up with the confederate Army, had ridden through the Cumberland Mountains. Since there were no hostels or inns, he had accepted the hospitality of mountain cabin homes. Two things had impressed him—the poverty of the mountain people and their high native intelligence. . . . Yet few of the mountaineers could even read or write. Schools and churches in these areas were almost nonexistent.

Then and there Dr. Guerrant made a solemn promise to God. "If I live through the war," he vowed, "I'll return to help these mountain people."

The vow was kept. In 1897, the little doctor gave up a fine medical practice at Mt. Sterling, Kentucky, in order to found the Society of Soul Winners, also known as the American Inland Mission. There were no funds to begin with. Dr. Guerrant's only capital was a dream in his heart and the faith that he was embarking on God's plan for his life. But ten years later, sixty-seven teachers and ministers were engaged in this work among the mountaineers: fifty-six churches, schools,

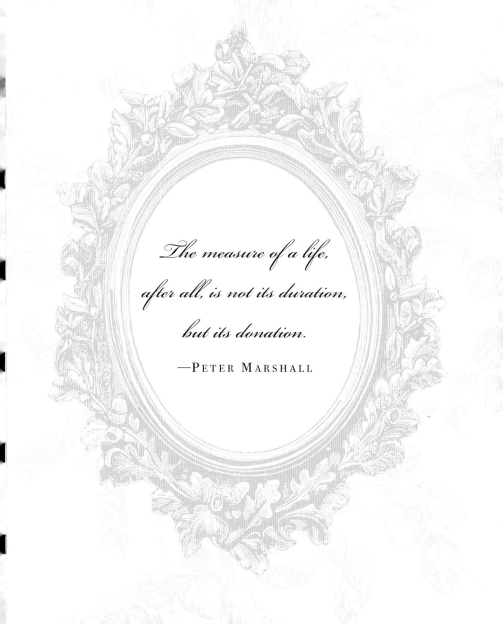

The measure of a life,

after all, is not its duration,

but its donation.

—PETER MARSHALL

As I sat by the window in Florida that March morning, my mind drifted back 73 years to a snowy afternoon in a tiny mountain town. . . .

I had volunteered to teach in a mission school up in the Great Smokies, an adventure that later inspired Catherine's novel, *Christy*. When I hugged my father good-bye in the grimy Asheville railroad station on that winter morning, he was wiping his eyes. He felt I was too young and inexperienced. I was only eighteen. But he didn't try to talk me out of it. Instead, he gave me courage. "Take these words with you," he said. "Take them to heart. They're from Isaiah 41:13, 'For I the LORD thy God will hold thy right hand, saying unto thee, fear not; I will help thee.'"

I whispered those words as I waved through the coach window until Papa was lost in the steam and smoke.

As I took my seat, I suddenly realized that I was hungry. It had been a long time since breakfast. I lifted the lid of the little wicker basket mother had given me. There was chicken breast and some thin buttered slices of salt-rising bread. There was an apple, several slices of spice cake, some Nabisco wafers, a small bottle of fresh buttermilk. As I munched on the chicken and bread, memories of home, which had already crowded dangerously close, came sweeping over me.

I thought of the big old kitchen—the stove with the warming oven above; the sink under the double windows; the tall spice cabinet with its pierced metal doors.... All of my childhood I had delighted in opening the doors of that spice cabinet just to whiff the wonderful fragrances. Why had smells— pleasant and unpleasant—always been so important to me? Sometimes the bad ones were torture, as on this trip. But then the nice ones more than made up for it—like the honeysuckle on the fence behind our house in late May; or in August the grapes hanging in heavy clusters on the trellised arbor-archway leading from the back porch to the coal house; or the fingers of fragrance that reached to every crevice of the house while mother's bread was baking.

I reached in the basket for the buttermilk and a cup. To my surprise, instead of the tin cup that I expected, I brought out a pink lustre one, part of my favorite childhood tea set. I found myself turning the cup over and over in my hands. It was beautiful. Thin, translucent pink.... Then I realized I was seeing the pink through a blur. So mother had wanted the cup to say something to me. Well, perhaps I was being foolish to leave my wonderful home. Or was I? I only knew that it was an experiment I had to make.

For in spite of the homesickness, I felt elation about being turned loose to make my own way in the world. I had sense enough to keep it strictly to myself, but secretly I was certain that I was about to take the world by storm.

—CRISTY HUDDLESTON
in *Christy*

It was snowing even harder when I finally stepped off the train at the little way station of Del Rio, Tennessee, expecting someone to meet me. But the snow-drifted platform was empty. I creaked open the door and hesitantly approached a man in a green eye-shade with mutton-chop whiskers who was taping a telegraph key.

Turning to me, he scratched his head and said: "Nope, nobody from the mission's been here." Then, looking at me closer through wire-rimmed glasses, he added, "But, I'll tell you, Miss, Mrs. Burnett across the way keeps boarders; you might be more comfortable there."

After picking my way across the tracks through the deepening snow, I knocked on Mrs. Burnett's paint-cracked door. It was pulled back by a heavy woman with a gray bun who ushered me inside.

The aroma of pot-roast filled the hall and she kindly invited me to join the others for dinner.

"What are you doing here in Del Rio?" she asked as I hung up my coat.

"I'm going to teach at the Ebenezer Mission School," I said.

She stared at me, hands on hips.

"You know what my advice is, little girl?"

"No," I replied, trembling.

"Have you ever lived where you wash clothes in a tub an' beat 'em with a stick?" She threw a look out the snow-encrusted window. "It's rough livin' up in those hills. My advice to you, little girl, is to get right back on the next train and go home."

I was mortified. Did I look that vulnerable? For a moment I wavered. Perhaps she was right. Home now seemed so safe and warm. And my parents would welcome me back.

Fear not, came the words, *I will help thee.*

I knew instinctively that the Lord's promise was not for those who gave up, but for those who forged ahead. Just as He guided the Israelites when they left Egypt to work their way through the wilderness, I knew He would guide me.

I looked up at the landlady and tried to keep my voice steady, "Mrs. Burnett, all I want to do is get out to the Mission in the morning."

She pursed her lips, then smiled, seeing, I suppose, that I meant business. The next morning she took me to the little post office where I met the mail delivery man.

"You can walk with me up to the Mission, if you like," he said, pulling on his boots. "It's seven miles."

The powdery snow was deep, but I trudged along with him carrying my bag.

It took all morning working our way along wind-whipped rocky ridges and slogging through shadowy hollows, but finally we reached the Ebenezer Mission.

The next day I was teaching in its one-room school, where I found the mountain children bright and inquisitive. Their minds were keen and they wanted to learn. Though I soon found myself in over my head, I kept my thoughts centered on God's great promise: *Fear not, I will help thee.*

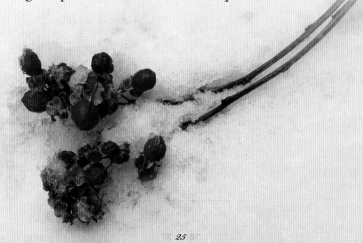

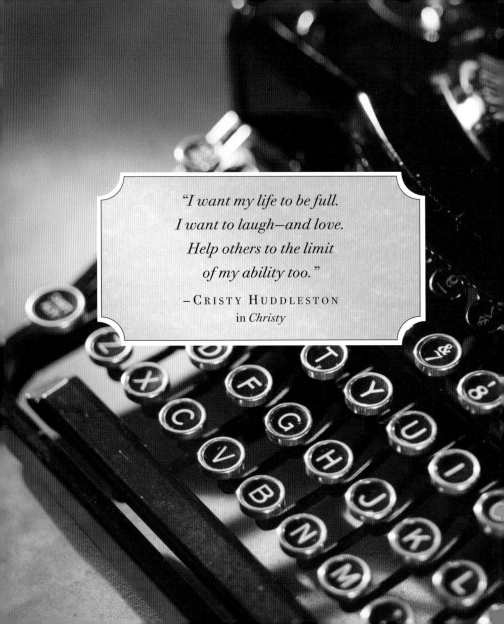

"*I want my life to be full.
I want to laugh—and love.
Help others to the limit
of my ability too.*"

–CRISTY HUDDLESTON
in *Christy*

We children loved the story of Mother and the big black hat.

It happened when she was just a girl of nineteen, teaching in the one-room Ebenezer Mission School. Mother was taller than average. . . . She had extremely large, expressive blue eyes and an aquiline nose with a piquant tilt at the end. Her chestnut-colored hair was so long she could sit on it. This she wore pinned up on top of her head in a modified pompadour.

Firmly fixed in Mother's mind was the thought that God loves beauty, (did He not create all beauty in the first place?) and that dowdiness dishonored Him.

There came the day when the Mission was in dire need of funds. Mother had received an invitation to speak in Knoxville to the Tennessee University Club and to the women of one of the churches. There was a good chance these organizations would help her meet the mission's emergency. In addition Mother planned to call on several Knoxville businessmen with a reputation for philanthropy.

For these speaking engagements and interviews, Mother was determined not to look like a mountain missionary who needed to beg for herself as well as for the mountaineers. . . .

A visit to a beauty parlor was her first step. She emerged with an elaborate hair-do, curls on top, a figure-eight in back.

Next she sought out one of the city's best stores. There Mother found an enormous black hat with sweeping ostrich plumes. It was extraordinarily becoming and would be perfect with her one good garment—a black broadcloth suit.

But the hat was priced at $25.00—every penny of her salary for one month. She pondered a long time. Should the $25.00 go directly into the mission fund, or would buying it actually be an investment in the work? Of course, in those days no well-bred woman went bareheaded into a public place. She had just about convinced herself that the hat was too expensive when she felt a strong "go-ahead" . . . and bought the hat.

Later that day, dressed to the hilt, her blue eyes sparkling with the fun of this feminine adventure, she swept into the downtown offices of Mr. Rush Hazen, a wholesale grocer and philanthropist.

Heads at rows of desks turned to stare. Even Mr. Hazen stared. In fact he all but whistled. "You—a missionary? I don't believe it. Why hasn't somebody thought of sending out missionaries like you before? What can I do for you?"

Mr. Hazen did a great deal. In the city of Knoxville his name was magic. Triumphantly Mother went back to the mission with enough food and money to keep boarding students all winter, plus the promise of more money for the future. She also went back more secure than ever in the conviction that with God, nothing is impossible.

A year [after coming to teach at the mission school], I came to another turn in the road. John Wood, a handsome young mission preacher with brown eyes and black hair asked me to marry him.

My new husband's first pastorate was the Meadow Creek Presbyterian Church in the Tennessee foothills. After a wonderful three years there, he was called to the little town of Umatilla, Florida, where we lived in a small rented house. The church wanted us to have a manse, and though John, a good carpenter, offered to build it, we needed materials.

At that time the famous William Jennings Bryan, who ran three times for the Presidency, was in the area. Someone suggested that if we could get him to speak, we could count on a sizeable collection. Well, I didn't know how to handle something big like that, and I was daunted by the prospect, so I put it all in God's hands.

Fear not, I will help thee.

I went to Ocala, a big town nearby, where Bryan, the Great Commoner, was speaking. As I was registering at the hotel, who should come to the desk but the tall, dignified Mr. Bryan and his entourage. I just turned, introduced myself, and invited him to speak at our church.

He smiled, bowed, and said: "I'll be at your house, Friday, Ma'am, for chicken dinner." Mr. Bryan was a man who dearly loved his victuals. Well, come he did and he was just wonderful. They didn't call him the Silver-Tongued Orator for nothing. He spoke right to my heart that hot afternoon when he said that if we really try to do the right thing, the circumstances of life tend to work together to promote the very thing we're trying to accomplish. As the Bible says, "All things work together for good to those who love God" (Romans 8:28).

Mr. Bryan also enjoyed my fried chicken, and we did have a good offering that helped us get the building materials. John worked all summer building that manse.

If we make our faith a natural part of the home and share Christ in all aspects of family life, the children should be open to it naturally by adolescence, the point at which they are capable of rational decision-making. But if we've skipped our day-to-day homework and then try to introduce what is really a foreign concept to the child, it's going to be hard.

—CATHERINE MARSHALL

My dear Mr. Rader:

Just wanted to let you know that we have a baby girl, who made her appearance on Saturday night at 12:20 a.m. She weighs 9½ pounds and mother and child are doing nicely.

Will see you all on the third Sunday Morning. Regards to all.

Yours truly,

John A. Wood

John A. Wood

A NOTE FROM
CATHERINE'S FATHER,
JOHN WOOD, ANNOUNCING
HER BIRTH ON
SEPTEMBER 27, 1914

Do not think me fanciful

too imaginative

or too extravagant in my language

when I say that I think of women,

and particularly of our mothers,

as Keepers of the Springs.

The phrase, while poetic, is true and descriptive.

We feel its warmth . . .

its softening influence . . .

and however forgetful we have been . . .

however much we have taken for granted

life's precious gifts

we are conscious of wistful memories

that surge out of the past—

the sweet tender poignant fragrances of love.

Nothing that has been said,

nothing that could be said,

or that ever will be said, would be eloquent enough,

expressive enough, or adequate to make

articulate that peculiar emotion we feel to our mothers.

—PETER MARSHALL

Leonora Wood and baby Sarah Catheri

I'll never know how even Mother's boundless energy covered all she did. In addition to everything else, she was a good cook. Her hot rolls were feathery-light. The cool pantry just off the kitchen had shelves always filled with canned cherries, apple butter, grape jelly, fig preserves, and bottles of homemade grape juice. Always there was a well-stocked cookie jar. On the screened-in back porch we made freezers of ice cream, and at green tomato time, tubs of chow-chow. Mother's boiled custard, smooth as a baby's cheek, was in the best Southern tradition, and Christmas was never complete without her fragrant mince-meat pies.

September 19, 1921

Today our dear little girl starts to school. No longer a baby, but in our hearts she will always be "just our baby."

Mingled with the pride and thanksgiving that fills the mother's heart there is an undercurrent of sadness—the little life's no longer wholly under the home influences. Other lives and other forces will henceforth influence the life.

But as this precious, pure little "Rose Bud" goes into the world, and day by day develops and unfolds, may its heart ever be turned toward the Sun of Righteousness and may its perfume never be tainted and spoiled by the things of the world. . . . This shall always be the prayer of the mother. My prayer will ever be given that you, dear child, may bless and beautify everthing that you touch.

Mother always believed in action; she was certain that idle children—hers or anyone else's—were headed for trouble. It was she who suggested that my brother and sister and I make a collection of butterflies and moths, plant a wild-flower garden, build a tree house.

Mother also headed the Girl Scout program for our West Virginia town—all six troops of us. She persuaded my good-natured father to go on camping expeditions (which he loathed), made him sleep on canvas cots in tents that often leaked, wade through mud, endure mosquitoes, warmed-over hot dogs and canned beans, and (what was worst of all to him) breathe the fumes of citronella. Father made endless jokes through it all.

Idle? Not a chance for any of us.

SARAH CATHERINE AND BABY SISTER EMMY

September 27, 1921

Seven years old today, seven years of childish joy, blessings and love. The sunshine of your Father's and mother's hearts . . . a "little light" to keep us in the path of righteousness.

May our dear Father lead you tenderly along life's pathway—and keep you always as sweet and pure and you are today is the prayer of your proud parents.

hen I was seven I acquired
German measles. During convalescence my mother
read to me that old [favorite] *The Five Little Peppers and
How They Grew.* One passage in the book entranced me
especially—the part about the Pepper family's Christmas.

Many years later I happened across the old book. Very curious
as to why this one passage had such a halo around it in my
memory, I reread the Christmas chapter. To my astonishment,
I found there was nothing very special about it.

The Pepper children were very poor. They had to
make every ornament for their tree. Bits of tinfoil
and bright paper were pasted over hickory nuts
to make balls. Candle ends were collected to
light the tree. Polly and Ben Pepper
popped popcorn, strung it, and wove it in

and out among the branches. . . . How well I remember being almost envious of the Pepper family's poverty.

What fun it would be, I thought, for a family to spend a whole evening together, stringing popcorn and making ornaments. Who wanted to *buy* Christmas tree ornaments? Who, indeed? Certainly no child. . . .

All children have this imaginative quality, along with a joyous ability to live in the present moment and a sharp sensitivity to a freshly beautiful world. It's as if a child savors life — sights, sounds, colors — fairly rolls it around her tongue. . . . .

But we never learn any of this until we spend extra time with our children. They, in turn, need that extra time, if we really want to give them happiness and lastingly joyous memories.

The speed and artificiality of the life most of us are living these days . . . almost stifles the imaginative creativity in our children. . . . That is why the most cherished gift we parents can give our children . . . is our time—ourselves. Nothing—no gift, no matter how expensive—can take the place of this.

Love springs

from giving,

even as giving grows

out of love.

—CATHERINE MARSHALL

A TRIBUTE FOR MOTHER FROM
CATHERINE'S SISTER, EMMY HOSKINS:

y most vivid memories of Mother are from when we lived in Keyser, West Virginia, where Dad was a pastor from 1924 to 1942. Mother, ever the organizer, had gone immediately to work with the Sunday school, which had a great many young people. She began with the primary department and went right up through the grades.

Five years after we arrived in Keyser, the great depression hit. . . . The chief industry was the railroad shops—the round-house where all the locomotives were serviced before starting the long pull over the mountains to Cincinnati. Probably five to six hundred men were working in the shops when the depression hit, at which time most of them lost their jobs. It was a very serious time. There were even people in our own congregation who were hungry.

Mother tried to help each needy family by gathering together food and clothing donated by friends and neighbors. Later in this period, my brother Bob and I were often pressed into service, loading the food and clothing into our stake wagon and pulling it to the family in need. . . .

The increasing number of poverty stricken families in Keyser troubled Mother greatly. It soon became apparent to her that an area called "Radical Hill," where several hundred families lived, was a slum area. She had to do something to help those people.

She enlisted the aid of some of the older youth of our church. . . . They started visiting each home on Radical Hill, taking a survey of the needs.

After each visit, Mother came home, sat at the table and cried. She said the conditions were unbelievable; they reminded her of the sad situations in Morgan Gap, Tennessee. . . .

There was a small house in the area that was rented for use as a community-type center. . . . A Sunday afternoon Sunday school was started and there were also classes started to teach the women how to sew and to practice better nutrition and hygiene. . . .

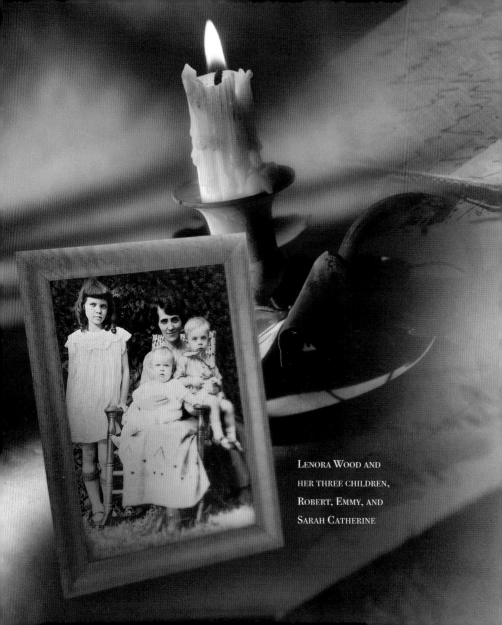

LENORA WOOD AND
HER THREE CHILDREN,
ROBERT, EMMY, AND
SARAH CATHERINE

Mother spoke about Radical Hill to the proper Keyser authorities. She said that the place couldn't be anything as long as it was called "Radical Hill" and that the town should immediately change its name. I don't recall who came up with the name "Potomac Heights," but soon that was how the area was known.

As a little girl, there were many times I resented all the time, energy, and love Mother gave to others, but the missionary spirit in her never died. Deep down I wouldn't have wanted it any other way . . . for it was that spirit that made Mother—well, Mother!

There is no question in

my mind, but that we are

our biggest and best selves

when we give ourselves to

the Lord to be used by Him,

and when His power is given

to us to be used in our work.

—LEONORA WOOD

It can be truthfully said that Keyser, West Virginia, is a small, friendly town, nestled close to the banks of the historic Potomac River, in a narrow green valley framed by the ruggedly beautiful Appalachian Mountains. It can also be just as truthfully said that Keyser is a whistle-stop town, crowded around the mainlines of the B & O Railroad, continuously blanketed under the black, grimy soot of soft coal smoke. . . .

Our new home, known and referred to by everyone as the Manse was a large, ten-room frame house built in the early nineteen hundreds. The house was set close to the street with a large side yard enclosed with a neatly trimmed privet hedge. Our huge back yard, with its lily pond, flower gardens, fruit trees, summer house and spacious lawn . . . became the neighborhood recreation area and the scene of many church picnics.

The interior of the house itself was very similar to many other houses of its period. It had a long center hall, large rooms with high ceilings and heavy inexpensive chandeliers, and an ornate stairway leading to another center hall upstairs. Yet the house had many of those unique rather impractical architectural innovations that made it a wonderfully exciting place for Bob, Em, and me. There were the gloomy winding backstairs, affording quick but not too silent escapes from the kitchen to the upper reaches of the house. There was the great attic with its many crevices full of exciting unexplored trunks and boxes. . . . There was the large kitchen pantry with the hidden and forbidden foods: cookies, spice cakes, canned cherries and apple butter, bottles of homemade grape juice and root-beer. There was the long stairway banister, built to simply invite sliding. There was the shady front porch for the long summer evenings of Parchesi and Caroms; the screened–in back porch for freezing ice cream and making tubs of chow-chow.

This was our house as I remember it—the house as I will always want to remember it.

January 2, 1924,
Wednesday evening

Our little girl, 9 years old, played the piano for prayer meeting. She loves hymns and plays nicely. Our hearts were filled with pride that our "wee girlie" could accompany so nicely. Her first hymn to play in public was "Jesus Loves Even Me."

Behind the old manse in Keyser, West Virginia ...
stood a grove of gnarled locust trees. Beside it
loomed a challenging looking mountain. The mountain, the locusts, and twelve years of happy family
living in that house left permanent impressions on
my life.

We moved into this ten-room frame house on
December 4, 1924. That afternoon we three children
stood in the middle of the welter of packing
boxes and brazenly pleaded for time out to
climb the mountain. In Mississippi we had
known delta country and mosquitoes; mountains
were entrancingly new to us.

"It is true," said Mother, thinking out loud, "that the trunk and barrels of china will not run away. For that matter, neither will Father nor the church. And you children could help me make the beds later."

We could see that she was rapidly weakening. We said lustily that we would just love to make the beds later——and were off.

Such a jaunt was altogether typical of Mother. She believed in doing housework when there was nothing more interesting to do. Things like talking or writing history, studying inscriptions on old tombstones, or organizing young people's work. Obviously, the hike came under the heading of young peoples' work.

I had been recovering from the measles. Then one morning when the measles spots had all but disappeared, mother discovered that I was coming down with chicken-pox. This was grossly unfair, and I wept.

"I'll read to you a lot," mother promised in desperation. "We'll make the time pass quickly. You'll see."

She was as good as her word. Looking back now, I know that our mother deliberately used these periods of childhood illnesses as veritable reading feasts, so much so that we remember these periods as some of the happiest times of our lives.

ur parents gave us all the freedom we needed to explore the countryside. In fact, Mother's attitude about walks, long hikes, camping trips and nature study aided and abetted our sense of adventure in all such explorations. In the early spring, even before the snow had completely melted, we and our playmates—the Fisher girls across the street and the Kerrykendall children—would climb Fort Piano to hunt for Trailing Arbutus. We knew that the long winter was really over when the wild crab apple burst into bloom, when the fields were starred with Hepaticas and pink and white Spring Beauties. There were secret places where purple and white violets grew in abundance. . . .

We were enchanted with some of nature's whimsies like Jack-in-the-Pulpits, Dutchman's Breeches, or the all-white ghostly Indian Pipes. We picked walnuts and chestnuts; tried smoking

Indian Stokies. We gathered bundle-shaped cocoons and kept them for months until shimmering green Lunas or velvety Crecropia moths emerged. We made prints of leaves with blue photographer's paper and calculated the age of trees by the rings of growth on the stumps. We experimented to see whether Dandelions and Crinkle Root really made good salads and whether we could make the root of the Bog Potato into cakes, as had the Indians.

It was Mother who suggested that we make a collection of butterflies and moths. Father made butterfly nets and wing-stretchers for us. For months the house smelled dreadful—of formaldehyde. We gamboled clumsily through the fields wielding the nets, climbed trees to collect hundreds of bundle-shaped cocoons, and watched breathlessly as it came time for the moths to emerge.

I still remember the delicate green of the shimmering Luna moths, surely one of the most beautiful greens on earth.

My brother collected rocks and arrowheads and pictures of pretty girls. We three children had a procession of dogs, canaries, and guinea pigs as pets. I had a wildflower garden. Father helped us build a croquet court, then strung lights in the backyard so we could invite our friends to play at night. We built a tree-house in the cherry tree and made a club house out of an old chicken house. Mother talked Father into building an elaborate summer house (it turned out to be fine for teen-age courting) and an outsized goldfish pond. We even started breeding rare species of tropical fish.

"It's today I must be livin'" . . .

Human life is short. Each of us has a limited number of years. So are we going to go through those so-few years with little time for our family and friends, with unseeing eyes for the beauties around us, concentrating on accumulating money and things when we have to leave them all behind anyway?

—CRISTY HUDDLESTON
in *Christy*

y brother claims that one of the happiest times of his childhood was a period when he had been exposed to scarlet fever, and he and Mother were quarantined. He had Mother all to himself. Her company was a pleasure; her conversation a delight. The hours of reading together, pure joy. What more could a boy ask?

The process of growing up seemed to be an uphill fight for survival for my young brother and sister. Bob always suffered most. While he and Em were sled-riding down a steep hill, they ran directly into an iron ash barrel that was frozen solidly to the ground. This cost Bob four front teeth, a smashed nose, and pulverized lips; Em was only bruised. Bob broke his arm learning to high jump; fractured several ribs skiing; stuck an ice pick through one hand. Regularly, each summer his eyes were swollen shut

BOB, MOTHER,
EMMY, AND
SARAH CATHERINE,
CIRCA 1921.

with poison ivy; each winter he contracted all the children's diseases going. No wonder Dr. Blanchard's little car was seen so often parked in the Manse driveway.

Mother and Dr. Blanchard became fast friends. On each visit, he would compliment Mother. "You've diagnosed it right again, Mrs. Wood. It *is* German measles. . . . It's wonderful the way you can combine medical knowledge with common sense."

We children were not as impressed as Dr. Blanchard because we didn't like the things mother attributed to her *common sense*—things like having to wear horrid long underwear and galoshes much too often. It seemed to us that the common sense had a tendency to become medical jags.

There was the Milk-of-Magnesia jag. For a while Mother designated Friday nights as "Milk of Magnesia night." This remedy she prescribed just on good general cleaning-out principles. . . . After that came the Argyrol period. Mother was sure that several drops of this dark brown liquid up our noses each morning would prevent winter colds. . . .

One morning our brother dawdled over his breakfast. The school bell had already rung. Bob had almost succeeded in giving Mother the slip and getting out the front door without the hated nose drops, when she caught him and called him back. She whisked him upstairs to the bathroom and hurriedly reached into the medicine cabinet. Grabbing a bottle with dark brown stains on its label, she squirted something up Bob's pug nose.

He let out a yell and started dancing wildly down the hall. He held his nose, screaming as he danced. Mother, startled by such a violent reaction, looked more closely at the bottle in her hand. It was Iodine! She had put Iodine up Bob's nose!

Really frightened, she yelled, "Great Caesar's ghost! Dad! Come quick!" Bob's screams already had Father coming—two steps at a time.

That day Dr. Blanchard didn't have much to say about Mother's fine medical common sense!

The tendency now is to give short shrift to home-making and children. That's a key problem—children aren't getting enough time from their parents. . . . And the problem is that a child will equate the love of God with how much real love he's getting from his parents. . . .

I had a father who gave us time—one of the hardest and most important things about parenting. It takes a lot of unselfishness. . . . I guarantee that without such a relationship a child will not be as good a marriage partner when he or she grows up. Children need the physical touch.

—CATHERINE MARSHALL

Father's book-lined study was the heart of our home. This is where the family always gathered in the evenings. While Mother mended or darned, and Father read, we children did our lessons. We would sprawl full length on the floor or sit at one of the pullout leaves of Father's rolltop desk, or in the old leather-covered Morris chair. . . . We never thought of reading, or paper work or even school work as any great chore, perhaps because our parents didn't ask us to go off by ourselves to our upstairs' bedrooms in order to concentrate. Rather, we found joy in studying, because it was fun to do with the family around us. In time, the warmth and coziness of the room where we studied seemed to become a part of the studying itself. Father and Mother were always near; there were shelves of books, . . . ferns, the birdcage with a singing canary, mother's rolls rising on the hot-air register, the shades drawn against a winter's night.

y mind slips back to the hard times, back to the days when we were living through the harsh financial struggles of the early thirties. At that time Father was a Presbyterian minister in a small West Virginia town. Because his church people were suffering so much financially, Dad had voluntarily taken three successive cuts in salary. That meant our family of five barely scraped along.

Dad's small check did not always last the week. When that happened, the Friday or Saturday grocery shopping had to include an element of acute embarrassment to us children. Even now my brother Bob tells me that he winces at the memory of seeking out our friend the grocer and saying with a lowered voice, "Dad said, if you'll bill him, he'll drop by Monday to pay you." (Father was handed his salary check on Sunday night.)

During this stretch of years our style of living changed in a number of ways. Our family had no car. We children bicycled; our parents walked. Bob and my sister Em and I went regularly to a neighbor's on Overton Place to read the voluminous Sunday funnies since one of our economies was cutting out the Sunday paper. And there was a particular brown-velvet dress Mother made for me out of someone's hand-me-down. The velvet was worn in places and the chocolate brown was wrong for a young girl. I think I suffered in silence, but I've never forgotten that dress.

Some of those things were difficult for us—we children certainly didn't enjoy them—yet we went through those bad Depression years unharmed, chiefly because no tinge of fear about lack of money ever entered our home. Much of this was because of Mother. I don't think it ever entered Mother's head that we were living through a period of poverty. She simply never saw it as that. She went through each and every difficult day of the Depression as though she had some secret bank account to draw from when we were in need—and in a sense she did—but her real secret was an attitude, her utterly confident approach to our condition.

We may have been hard-pressed, we may have done without all luxuries, but Mother always provided us with a feeling of well-being. One way she did this was the ingenious manner in which she contrived to give to others. Out of our meager pantry she would send a sick neighbor a supper tray of something delicious she had prepared—velvety-smooth boiled custard, feather-light homemade rolls—served up on our best china and always with a dainty bouquet from our garden.

Or take the matter of mush. We were reduced to eating this cornmeal staple frequently because there was no money for meat. But we children didn't mind at all—not the way Mother made it: sliced thin, browned crisply, and served with maple syrup. Mother could make mush into an occasion. And she even managed to give that away. Somehow she discovered that Mr. Edwards, our wealthy

LEONORA AND
JOHN WOOD WITH
THEIR CHILDREN

neighbor, was as fond of mush as we children were. But his wife never served him such lowly fare. So from time to time he would be the grateful recipient of hot, golden-fried mush. "Poor Mister Edwards," we'd say, truly in sympathy.

Only subconsciously were we aware of it, but Mother was providing us constantly with an object lesson in giving. The message: No matter how little you have, you can always give some of it away. And when you can do that, you can hardly consider yourself poor.

But there was even more to it than that. For Mother, giving was an act of faith, and the spiritual principle of giving out of scarcity came as easily to her as if she had invented it. Whenever we saw an old-fashioned pump in a farm-yard, we knew what she'd tell us. "If you drink the cup of water that's waiting there, you can slake your own thirst, but if you pour it in the pump and work the handle, you'll start enough water flowing to satisfy all our thirsts." She likened the principle of priming the pump to God's own law of abundance.

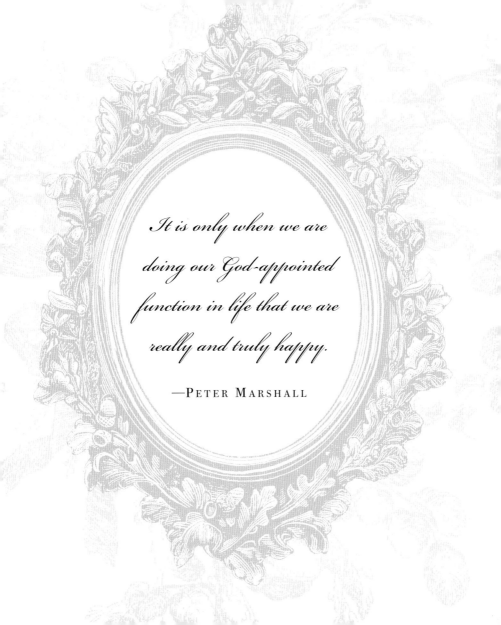

*It is only when we are
doing our God-appointed
function in life that we are
really and truly happy.*

—PETER MARSHALL

Sarah Catherine,
High School graduation

We hear about every other kind of women—

beautiful women,

smart women,

sophisticated women,

career women,

talented women, . . .

but so seldom do we hear of a godly woman.

—PETER MARSHALL

One of the most provocative facts I know is that every man-made object, as well as every event in your life and mine, starts with an idea or a picture in the mind. My mother first taught me this, and at the same time she vividly demonstrated to me the prayer that helps dreams come true.

In my teens I had long had the dream of going to college. But this was Depression time and the church my father served as minister was suffering financially too. I was accepted at Agnes Scott College, in Atlanta, had saved some money from debating prizes, had the promise of a work scholarship—yet we were still several hundred dollars short.

One evening Mother found me lying across my bed, face down, sobbing. She sat down beside me. "You and I are going to pray about this," she said quietly.

We went into the guest room and knelt beside the old-

fashioned, golden oak bed, the one that Mother and Father had bought for their first home. "I know it's right for you to go to college," Mother said. "Every problem has a solution; let's ask God to tell us how to bring this dream to reality." And so we knelt by the bed and prayed about it.

I shall never forget that evening. During those quiet moments in the bedroom, I was learning what faith is and how it works. It is true that my faith was immature and weak, but the strength of Mother's was contagious. She had helped me take my first step in faith. The answer would come. We knew it would, though neither of us had any idea how.

When it came, it was the offer of a job for Mother with the Federal Writer's project. Would she be willing to write the history of the county? Would she! Her salary would cover the amount needed for my college expenses with a little to spare.

LETTERS TO SARAH CATHERINE ATTENDING COLLEGE IN GEORGIA

My precious Girlie:

. . . We were sorry to see from your letter yesterday that you were blue. I know how you felt, with the other girls getting [to go] home, and being away from home and without any money. But darling child, I hope all this has passed and that you are feeling your dear sweet self again. Some day things will all work out right for us. We are not going to fret and worry. Things may be topsy-turvy in this old world, but we know that our heavenly Father is our FATHER and that He will guide us and take care of us. Each morning when Daddy and I have prayers we just commit you into His keeping, and ask that in every way that you maybe taken care of. . . .

Your family loves you with all their hearts.

Mother

9-14-32

My precious Girlie:

We are just so happy to know you are at school
and everything so pleasing. . . .

Janet was singing your praises last night,
and said "I have no fear but that Sarah
Catherine will make her mark in the world."

I send a big heart full of love for you my
darling big girl. You are the joy of our lives
and we always thank the Lord for keeping you
so sweet and good.

Your devoted,

Mother

Dearest daddy and mumsy,

I have a little while before lunch, so will
write you now. I have so much to tell you,
that I scarcely know where to begin. I don't
think I have ever had so much happen in a
single weekend in my life. . . . I suppose you
have guessed by now. It is all about the
Englishmen. . . .

The tea was lovely. Their home is awfully
nice, not elaborate, but just home-like. It was
very informal. In the living-room were lots of
books and flowers and lamps, a grand piano, and
best of all a huge beautiful fireplace. So you
can imagine what a marvelous time we had with
good tea, all sorts of little cakes and candy,
witty, brilliant conversation, music, and the
fireplace . . .

David walked home with me and got very,
very serious, so it is perhaps just as well

that they have gone today. I don't mean that he tried to kiss me or anything like that. He did say, however, that out of all the girls he had met in America, he would remember me. . . . Incidentally, he is one of the most attractive men I have ever met.

Perhaps you can imagine how I expanded almost out of myself this weekend. It is a very, very rare experience for me to find a man with whom I can not only be absolutely myself, but actually have to stretch to keep pace with him. . . .

I am very much afraid that by this time you are very much bored by such a lengthy letter, but I just had to tell you about it all. . . . Loads and loads of love for the sweetest family in the world.

Lovingly,

Sarah Catherine

March 4, 1934

I have been nearly crazy over my student budget. I had a letter from mother saying they simply couldn't pay it [$15.00] until April 1st. I cried after I read that letter—for the first time in many a day. I immediately sat down and wrote home again. I thought perhaps I hadn't made it strong enough. I filled four pages of pleading and sent it "special delivery."

I feel like my whole happiness depends on that reply. It would nearly kill me to have to go to Dr. Hayes and tell him I couldn't debate because I don't have $15.00. Every time I think of the fact (which is very often) that the answer to that letter may be "no" again, I have an awful sinking feeling in my stomach. Perhaps I am overestimating all this. Perhaps this time next year it will mean nothing in my life—but it means everything now.

A LETTER FROM MOTHER

My precious Girlie:

Well, mother has been considerably worried
about the money for your Student Budget and the
$75.40 due Mr. Tart. But while we call upon the
Lord, He answers. . . . I called Mrs. Macdonald
. . . and she said they would loan me the $10.00
for your student budget. Checks for both these
things will be in the mail in the morning. . . .

My dear child, it means just this, the Lord
never fails His trusting children, but we must
do our part and while we are struggling through
these trying times we must remember that we
have to save everything that we can. That only
the really essential things count. I want you
to buy your ticket for the seasons concerts and
lectures, but when it comes to the weekend
trips you will have to forgo these unless something happens that we have more money than we
have now. . . .

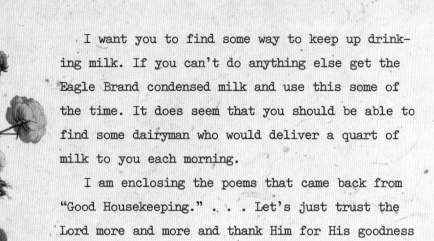

I want you to find some way to keep up drinking milk. If you can't do anything else get the Eagle Brand condensed milk and use this some of the time. It does seem that you should be able to find some dairyman who would deliver a quart of milk to you each morning.

I am enclosing the poems that came back from "Good Housekeeping." . . . Let's just trust the Lord more and more and thank Him for His goodness to us.

Devotedly,

Mother

My precious Big Girlie;

This is a glorious morning up here in the mountains. Just cool enough to make us feel like working. I hope you are having a nice day down there and that you are feeling fine.

We are mailing you, this morning, a box: your birthday cake, some mints, and a box of pencils etc. Do hope the cake will reach you in good shape. Daddy has tried very hard to fix it in the box so it would not move around and get crushed. We thought it would be nice for you to have this cake box to keep in your room. . . .

I hope your birthday will be a happy one. We will be thinking of you and praying for you, as we always are. You know how good we love you. . . .

Your devoted,

Mother

September 27, 1934

My birthday, and it has been a wonderful day. First, I got a sweet letter from precious Mumsey and a package with two skirts to wear to school. . . . Then this evening Lilly brought me three gorgeous dahlias and Shirley a bottle of Evening in Paris perfume. I tried to study tonight but couldn't, I was so happy.

I was a wee bit depressed by the number of candles on my cake—20 of them! I hate to leave my teens behind me. That somehow means leaving girlhood itself behind and falling heir to responsibilities and cares....Still...life is wonderful.

Dearest family:

This morning, in spite of the fact that Peter was away, and that it was dark and dreary and raining, Lib and I went to S. S. and church at Westminister. It wasn't as good as usual, of course, with Peter away. . . .

Mother, you guessed right about Peter. . . . You see the trouble is that as far as he's concerned, he doesn't know I exist. I have been suffering agonies for the past few weeks. I tell myself I'm silly, foolish, stupid every-thing, and it doesn't help a bit. . . . If I ever needed you, I do now. I'm telling you this, because I want you to know it and anyway perhaps you have some good advice. You always do. And don't tell me to stay away from the church, because I simply couldn't. . . .

I don't blame Peter at all. Anyone in his position has to be awfully impersonal. . . .

But if he only knew all the agony I have been going thru. Mother, I wish you were here. Don't worry though, because I haven't lost my head at all and as long as I still can use it I'll pull out. . . .

Loads and loads of love. Forgive your silly little girl. I'm such a doggone mess at times. I love you though!

Sarah Catherine

2-20-34

My dear Sarah Catherine:

. . . . I am much interested in what you have told
me about Peter Marshall. In fact, I am getting a bit
anxious lest you be falling in love with the man, or
at least with what you think he is. He sounds like
a man that it would not be hard to fall in love
with, but go slow, little girl, go slow. When the
right man comes along I haven't a doubt but that you
will fall, but I don't want you to make any mistakes
in this matter of the heart, see? Well, any way, I
am glad that you have found a place where you enjoy
Sunday school and church and I hope more, that you
will find some church work that you can do. It does
my heart good to know that you are interested as you
are in saving souls. . . . .

Heart's dearest love for you, my darling girl.
Mother lives her life over through you. It's a
great game, this game of living.

Mother

Spring, 1935

Dearest dad and mumsy,

I can't make this very long, but I do have
things to tell you.

At last my long-standing desire of some two
years has been fulfilled and I am going to have
a date with Mr. Marshall. I really didn't ever
think that would happen. It seems sort of like
a dream or a fairy tale. . . .

Even if nothing comes of this after this
date at least I'll have the consolation that I
could get at least one date out of the only man
I have really ever wanted one out of. . . .
He's the only man (to date) in my life that I
have been in the least attracted to. The point
is for me to try to keep myself from falling
in love with him, which (I am warning you)
would be very, very easy. He's a honey in every
way as far as I know. . . .

Well, I must stop. I just had to tell you about it. A date with him is one of the few things I have really wanted in my life and now I actually have it. Oh Boy! Oh Boy!

With much, much love,

Sarah Catherine

Monday Morning 5-13-35

My dear Sarah Catherine,

Your good letter came this morning. And I am
glad you tell me how you feel about everything. I
just wish, however, that you would not worry at
all about the matter of Peter. I believe with all
my heart that things of this kind are planned for
us, and that if it is the best for you. . . . if
he is THE ONE, that not only you, but he will know
it. And everything will work out as it should.
Just don't allow yourself to fret over it. Place
the whole thing in the Lord's hands, be willing to
be and do what He would have you. It will all work
out right. In the next place, I must confess that
the whole thing seems providential. . . .

Hearts dearest love,

Mother

My precious Girlie:

It is strange but in you I live again. I
have the joy over and over as I live through
experiences with you of realizing dreams that
have been locked up in my heart all of my
life. You'll have no trouble making me understand how you feel, and I'll be back of you
every step of the way.

Mother

On May 30th, we left for Decatur, Georgia to attend the graduation exercises; June 2, 1936, at Agnes Scott College. Really one of the big events in our family history, our little girl's graduation. Robert and Emma Lynn greatly enjoyed the trip and had their first taste of campus life. The girls, Sarah Catherine's friends, were lovely to them and the three days at college were an endless picnic.

Peter Marshall was also taken into our family group at this time and the children were quite annoyed that their "big sister" had so much time to spend with him. They had come all the way from West Virginia for this occasion and were being cheated.

I know that all of life is a question of stages, and that all of us go through a series of processes. I am perfectly certain that with our children we have to be patient enough, even in relation to our prayers concerning them, to give them and God time to work out these processes.

—CATHERINE MARSHALL

The world has enough women
who know how to be smart.

It needs women who are willing to be simple.

The world has enough women
who know how to be brilliant.

It needs some who will be brave.

The world has enough women
who are popular.

It needs more who are pure.

We need women, and men too, who would rather
be morally right than socially correct.

—Peter Marshall

MRS. CATHERINE MARSHALL

Dear Family,

. . . We're having a grand time—both of us resting a lot. Peter had a wire yesterday saying he had been finally extended the call to pastor the New York Avenue Presbyterian Church. Somehow it is beginning to look as though it is inevitable that we end up in Washington. They were perfectly lovely to us. . . .

We've had a grand time since we've been here—just doing whatever we please. Have seen "Romeo and Juliet" on the screen and Helen Hayes in "Victoria Regina" on the stage. . . . Both were grand. . . .

How can I thank you all darlings for everything. Every detail [of the wedding] went beautifully. Nothing could have been better and it is all a memory never to be forgotten.

Much love till I see you.

Devotedly,

Sarah Catherine

woman's true satisfactions have always been rooted in relationships rather than in accomplishment. That is why love is so necessary to our happiness. Always we've gotten more delight from people than from abstract ideas. Always we're looking for the human-interest story behind the façade. . . .

It's in this direction of an interest in people that fulfillment lies. Perhaps our grandmothers knew a secret here that women of this century need to rediscover. Because they thought of the guidance and development of their families as the most important thing in the world, homemaking turned out to be a big adventure rather than a chore. Precisely the same principles hold for the business world or community life or church work. How can even an ordinary person be jaded with life when extraordinary things are happening through her?

Dearest Family,

. . . We had an awfully nice Christmas, although a very quiet one. Miss Mary, as you know . . . was here with us, and I supposed we shall never know what real pleasure it gave her to be here. And Peter enjoyed all of it so much. Perhaps it was the first real Christmas that he has ever known. He bought a little tree which we put in the bay window and decorated simply with blue lights and icicles. . . .

We had a turkey, which was given us, fruit cocktail, mashed sweet potatoes flavored with orange juice served in orange rinds, green beans with mushrooms, cranberry sauce and ice cream and cake. Everyone testified to the fact that it was really a good dinner. Peter was the proudest host I have ever seen. He was so thrilled over being able actually to entertain his friends in his own home.

But I haven't told you about my gifts. He gave me a blue silk umbrella (which I very badly needed), and a locket (gold) which belonged to his mother. He is reputed to have cut his baby teeth on it . . . and his mother gave it to him when he came to this country. . . . He had it polished and cleaned up and his picture put in it. He also gave me a narrow white gold bracelet set with three small diamonds. He plans to add a diamond each birthday or anniversary. It is quite a lovely thing. . . . I gave him a leather brief case (I was sick of looking at the old one) . . . and a ridiculous mechanical clown who turns flips. . . .

Dearest, dearest love to the sweetest family in the world. I love you all.

Devotedly,

Sarah Catherine

Long before Wee Peter was born, his father [Peter Marshall] had become fond of A. A. Milne's Christopher Robin and Pooh Bear stories. In fact, during Peter's Atlanta ministry he had even managed to work some of this material into children's sermonettes. . . .

Peter had no difficulty whatever in transferring this affection for Christopher and Pooh to our son. Pooh (who could eat his way with ease through fourteen pots of honey), Eeyore, Tigger, Heffalump and the others were soon household pets. From hundreds of hours of reading Pooh aloud, I can shut my eyes and still see the delight of a small face under blond curls over something like Winnie-the-Pooh getting stuck in rabbit's hole.

"*Books are like friends.*
We must treat
them like friends."

—CRISTY HUDDLESTON
in *Christy*

ver and above running our ten-room house, feeding and medicating her family, keeping us in clean cloths, attending church meetings, and visiting the sick, Mother had to find time for her own favorite hobby—history.

West Virginia's horizons were steeped in historical lore. Mother took full advantage of living in the midst of it. She wrote endless articles. . . . She even wrote the history of B. C. Barnhouse. The initials in Barnhouse's name were significant. He was doing all right because he was then 113 years old. That fascinated mother.

Sometimes it seemed to us children that the older people were or the longer they had been dead, the more exciting they seemed to Mother. She would go to almost any lengths to study inscriptions on old tombstones. Sometimes she would take us

with her, such as on that trip to get the story on John Custis—
Martha Washington's father-in-law. Mother liked him because he
had been buried . . . standing straight up. Mother pointed out to
us that he had said he'd never bowed his head to any living person
in life, and he certainly wasn't going to do any bowing in death.

By the time Peter Marshall allied himself to the family,
Mother and her tombstones had become a family joke. Peter took
up the joke with gusto. It was he who introduced Mother to a
section of the country new to her—New England. That did it!
There are so *many* graveyards in New England. As we would be
driving through a village where the cemetery was four times as
populous as the village, Mother would inevitably say, "Isn't that
appalling!" So her son-in-law started calling them "Appallings."
"Mother," he would say, "just look at that Appalling. I know
you'll want to see that one. Tell you what—we'll just leave you
and pick you up this afternoon."

But Mother's sense of humor has never been her strongest
characteristic. In fact, it's nonexistent. So she could never appreciate Peter's witticisms quite as much as the rest of the family.

One night in Washington, I sat down in the living room of my home and had a long talk with a man who has known where he wanted to go in life, for a long time. I had not seen him in many years. He was wearing an unobtrusively expensive suit and had a debonair air of prosperity about him. He was here in the United States briefly from Austria. . . .

As I looked at Ray I saw living proof that dreams do come true. For Ray came from the wrong side of the tracks in a dirty little West Virginia town on the edge of the coal mines. He had been adopted by poor, uneducated people.

Dressed in working clothes and knee-length clodhoppers, Ray used to come to talk with my mother. He was always clean, but he didn't even own a suit of clothes. He would sit on the top step of our vine-shaded front porch talking . . . talking . . . while Mother sat in a wooden rocker shelling peas or stringing beans or darning socks. Mother soon saw his boundless energy and fine mind.

On one particular afternoon there emerged for Ray the same clear-cut idea I had always had—college. Once his dream was out in the open, standing there shimmering, poised in the air, Mother was delighted to see the wistfulness in Ray's brown eyes replaced by a kindling hope.

"But how can I manage it?" the boy asked. "I've no money saved. Nor any prospects.". . .

"Raymond, whatever you need, God has the supply ready for you, provided you're ready to receive it." Mother responded. "And ours is still a land of opportunity. The sky's the limit!"

For a preacher's wife who had little enough herself, this was a doughty philosophy. But Mother believed it and had often proved it so. . . .

So, with nothing but a flat wallet and faith in his dream, Raymond Thomas went off to college. How he made a great success of his life is much too long to chronicle here. It involved Mother's finding a woman to start him off with a loan . . . Mother writing him encouraging letters . . . Mother praying. And Raymond himself accepting responsibility, developing initiative. In four years he had twelve jobs, budgeting time as well as money. . . . It was a proud day for Mother when Ray received his degree, *cum laude*.

Years later, after earning a Ph.D. and traveling in over sixty countries with the U. S. Atomic Energy Program, with awe in his voice, Ray said to me, "To one women I owe the key to life. That woman is your mother."

Marriage to Peter Marshall
postponed the fulfillment of Catherine's dream
of becoming a writer. Then within
a year of his untimely death at age forty-six,
God rekindled the dream in her heart.
In the late fall of 1949, Catherine signed
a contract with Fleming Revell to publish the
first of her many successful books.

Catherine sent the following four
letters to her parents from Hollywood
in the 1950s, during the filming of the movie
based on her novel *A Man Called Peter*.
She also attended a book signing in Hollywood
for two of her smaller books: *God Loves You*
and *Let's Keep Christmas*.

Dearest mother and dad,

. . . We began our first real story confer-
ence at 10:30. . . . I began to feel that God
wanted me to suggest to Sam that we have a
little prayer before we began today. I wasn't
at all sure that I'd have the courage to suggest
it, but the idea stuck, and I knew it was right.
So I did—and there, very quietly sitting in his
office, with Sam and the scriptwriter, and a
secretary taking notes I prayed. I asked God to
bless the whole project, and to pour His ideas
through each of us, to pick the cast, and make
it His picture. Sam was awfully impressed, and I
know really glad that I did it.

As a result, we really had a fine day. . . .

Lovingly,

S.C.

Dearest mother and dad,

. . . I have lots of news and hardly know
where to begin. This last week has been a week
of meeting celebrities. On Sunday evening Mr.
and Mrs. Engle took me to dinner. First they
took me to see their home. They live up on one
of the hill-tops in a house distinctly Early
American in influence, but with large windows.

. . . One of the curious things out here is
how much Early American there is in interior
decorating. Perhaps it is an instinctive urge
to find a little stability in an atmosphere
that is anything but that. Mrs. Engle has large
braided rugs and all, but it's very tasteful
and homey, and of course, pretty lavish.

At the restaurant—one of the famous eating
places—Fred Allen, Gracie Burns and her husband
were sitting right at the next table. At a table
just across the aisle was Carey Grant. . . .

On Monday night I went to the Hollywood Christian group and made a talk. Mrs. Roy Rogers came for me and brought me home, so we had a good chance to talk. She is young looking, younger than I had thought she would be. . . . She and Roy Rogers are real sure 'nough Christians. It goes mighty deep with them and is utterly sincere—the real thing. Roy Rogers now includes in all his cowboy programs a plea for the children to go to Sunday school.

When I got to the meeting . . . Jane Russell was there, with two of her actress friends. They had to leave though, so did not hear my talk. She is beautiful alright. . . .

I long to hear from Peter [John] directly. . . . I too feel that this may be a pretty long-drawn-out thing, with several trips out here. I don't relish it in the least—but here I am. In the meantime, I do really think that God sent Peg to me for this time [to care for Peter John]. . . .

My dearest love to you both.

Leonora and John Wood

in the early 1950's

Sunday afternoon

Dearest mother and dad,

Yesterday it rained cats and dogs all day
the first rain they have had in months. . . .

I took a cab to the Studio and they loaned
me a Lincoln. . . . Then I found my short
evening dress yesterday, and it really is
lovely. . . . It is a medium blue lace with
little clusters of sequins scattered here and
there. It has long sleeves and a slightly
off-the-shoulder neckline, otherwise very
plain. I fell in love with it, and knew it
was my dress. . . .

The right people are being sent by God at just
the right time, as I knew they would be. . . .

Dearest love,

SC

Monday evening,

Dearest mother and dad,

I am awfully tired this evening, since I have practically spent the day at the autograph party at Robinsons—a big department store downtown. . . . The party was quite a success. They ran out of GOD LOVES YOU and LET'S KEEP CHRISTMAS, and I was kept busy continuously with never a breather.

We are planning on finishing up at the Studio on Friday and then I think I will take a little trip Saturday and Sunday and start home on Monday. . . .

Thursday night Dr. Edgar J. Goodspeed, who translated the Goodspeed Bible . . . is having a dinner party for me. And it's a formal, if you please. So I shall get to wear my new dress and Anita's little ermine jacket, and will surely be more dressed up than I have ever been in my life. . . .

I'll turn in for now. Dearest love to both of you.

Love,

Catherine

Dearest Catherine,

I did so much appreciate your good Mother's Day letter. It was just what I needed. I had rather have you and your love than all the gifts in the world. Few mothers have been so blessed, and I am more grateful than I can say for you and the things that you stand for.

Mother

Viewing the way I have traveled the last few years, I know now that if we parents want to get on with God's plan for us, only one way is open: commitment to marriage and to parenthood as a vocation. No ducking out, no fleeing, no excuses.

—CATHERINE MARSHALL

January 1960

Dear Dr. Dan,

Last November—when Len LeSourd and I stood
in the little Leesburg (Virginia) Presbyterian
Church and made our solemn, yet joyous wedding
vows—I knew that our new life would necessitate
rethinking many things. Among them has been the
matter of what portion of my writing career can
now continue and at what pace. As you know,
before my marriage I was well into the writing of
a novel, a project that I still want to complete.

Along with you, I believe that for a woman
the career of wife and mother always should have
priority. Surely the nurture of the Christian
home is all-important. And while Peter John has
now all but flown the nest (being a Junior at

Yale), Len and I still have three younger children, two sons and one daughter at home.

Naturally I could not have anticipated this drastic change in my life in 1958 when I joined the CHRISTIAN HERALD staff as Woman's Editor. This work has given me great joy because CHRISTIAN HERALD readers welcomed me with enthusiasm and have been most responsive to my articles. Therefore, though it appears unwise for me to continue in the post of Woman's Editor, I am loathe to give up writing for CHRISTIAN HERALD.

I suggest then that—for the present—I reduce my pace to that of a contributing author . . . . I feel that our readers will understand fully the necessity for this decision.

My warmest good wishes to you and CHRISTIAN HERALD always.

Sincerely,

Catherine Marshall LeSourd

od wants our happiness but He is forever reminding us that our happiness can never be had apart from our becoming mature people.

Part of that maturity is making the right choices. At the few times when I had most keenly felt the Reality that is God, I had known that He was offering me a choice. He would never violate my freedom of will.

The choice He was presenting to me now, [to love not only Len but his young daughter and two young sons as well], was suddenly painfully clear. To say "Yes" to the heartstream of life meant painful adjustment, involvement. I saw that if I chose the other road, I would be turning away from the main stream of life. That way would be comfortable, but it would also mean the slow softening deterioration of self-center. . . .

These insights turned out to be right, of course. When

romance comes into one's life with three children tagging along, it is not all moonlight and glow. Our new family requires a large house and a big yard. Dust and clutter accumulate in the house; moles burrow in the yard and dine on my best spring bulbs.

There have been battles with the daughter who is trying to grow up too soon—over nylons and makeup and the height of heels on shoes. . . . I have just answered the phone to be informed that Chester's restless throwing arm has gotten him in trouble again. He has been shooting peas using passing cars as a target. . . .

Bootsy, the miniature collie, got sick yesterday on the hall carpet. The day before that I spent minutes and minutes extracting Jeffrey's upset bag of popcorn from between the strings of the grand piano. I railed against the wasted time as I thought of the paragraphs of deathless prose I could have been turning out—and then laughed at myself.

As always, God had planned a much richer, fuller answer to prayer than I could have planned. Romance? Yes—wonderful romance. But also life with a capital L because it has a growing edge.

*What could be better calculated
to teach patience than trying to drum
manners or tidiness into children?*

—CATHERINE MARSHALL

Jesus is the only person who has the right to be put on a pedestal. If we climb down off of the pedestal and are real, we can save our children a lot of heartbreak and disillusionment. Put yourself on a pedestal in the home and you invite tragedy. But when parents are transparent, they set the right example. The child should see a pattern of openness, confession, and the immediate seeking of forgiveness from the Lord.

—CATHERINE MARSHALL

A find the rearing of children one of life's most turbulent and zany pursuits. Take a typical morning in our suburban household as of two years ago. Jeffrey was then 8; Chester, 11; Linda, 15; Peter, 24. Peter had graduated from Yale, then from Princeton Seminary, and had been at home for a time awaiting a call to a church.

We were awakened on that particular morning by a commotion in the boys' bedroom. A loud yelp took me there on the run. Chester complained, "Jeff bit me." Sure enough there were teeth marks on Chester's leg. . . .

At that moment Linda appeared in the hallway in her night clothes, a dazed, sleepy look on her face, her feet bare. "Linda, the floor is cold. Put on your slippers."

"Can't Mom. I put them in the washing machine and they shrank."

Obviously it was to be "one of those mornings." . . . Jeff dripped jam on his freshly pressed school pants and had to change them. Peter John called out that he had a dental appointment in New York and couldn't find any clean shorts. The three younger children dashed for the bus, banging the door behind them. Through the window I saw that they had made the bus. I turned around to pour myself a second cup of coffee, and there on the kitchen counter was Jeff's lunch. . . . .

I sank into the nearest chair, desperately needing that cup of coffee. As I sipped, trying to get back some calmness and perspective, in my mind I was addressing the Almighty: "Lord, what *is* this about anyway. When You put people together in families, just what *did* You really have in mind?"

Although the answer was not immediately forthcoming, it has been gradually dawning. . . . Day by day my suspicion grows that this family-life bit is one of the Creator's most sneaky tricks. For now I know: the family is the training ground—the testing center—where sinners get on with the painful process of being pummeled into saints. I fear that God is not half so concerned with our being what we call "happy" in this life (in His eyes, happiness never is an end in itself anyway, but a dividend) as in our being hammered and chiseled and molded into the characters He meant us to be all along.

And what is the most sure-fire method of rubbing off rough edges, forging us, shaping and molding us? Yes, you guessed. Parents rubbing against children; children bowing the will to parental authority as training for that bowing to God's authority. . . . Children learning to get along with one another. . . . For whether we like it or not, the Creator insists that we get on with being "members one of another." And if we cannot manage this in small family units, by what perverse reasoning do we imagine that we can succeed at it in the nation and across the world?

Perhaps the young will always be

extremists. Ours at any rate—from Peter

John right on down to the youngest—are

continually making clear to us how much

they scorn nice, safe, nominal gestures

toward religion. Instead, they are often

out in front pointing the way to a more

daring faith for us parents.

—CATHERINE MARSHALL

A Mother's Day card from
Catherine's daughter-in-law Edith

I've had such need for your special kind of mothering and you really have pulled through! You're very, very special to me and my heart is full of gratitude just thinking about what God has done for us. I love you!

—Edith

A Mother's Day greeting from
Catherine's son Chester LeSourd

Mom,

We always will remember you for things you have done for us. We love you always. Mom I really love you and thank you for the places you have carted me—to ballgames and practices—and for all the help and love you've given me in school work and when I'm sick. I just could not live without a mother who is as kind and understanding as you are.

Love, Chester

Letter to Catherine from her son Jeff LeSourd

5/11/78

Mom,

I am really looking forward to being with you this summer. I have learned so much by watching you and how you always strive to do your best in everything. I know that I have learned a lot of neat things from you. I try to find out why things work the way they do and this curiosity was kindled by you. A lot of my characteristics or traits I can credit to you because of the way that you have raised me.

When I see my fellow classmates here at college I realize how privileged I am to have such a wonderful family. I know how much you love me by the way that you have raised me. That means more to me than almost anything else in my life. I can never repay the debt I owe you. Whatever I may do with my life I know that you will be the main person who helped me become the person that I am. . . . I love you more and more each year. Thank you for your love for me.

Love always, Jeff

Rearing children and bringing them

up "in the nurture and admonition

of the Lord" is not only a full-time

responsibility of any parent but is

also the greatest witnessing field

and mission field in the world.

—CATHERINE MARSHALL

"*There's only one way to give advice to the young:
give it, and then be perfectly unconcerned as to
whether they take it or not. God alone is capable
of managing other people— even our own children.*"

—MISS ALICE
in *Christy*

A LETTER TO CATHERINE FROM HER DAUGHTER, LINDA LeSOURD

Mom,

This has been a glorious Christmas and glorious Fall for our relationship. . . . I sense so much more love and genuine warmth growing between us, for which I'm very grateful. You mean so much to me and I've longed for a good rapport between us. . . .

Mom, I want you to know that I appreciate the trouble you go to at Christmas, the love and the care and the thought you put into your gifts . . . and all you do to make this a special time of year. Being here now is the nicest Christmas present you all could give me. For that and for all the others—material and otherwise—I thank you.

Much, much love,

Linda

ome time ago a good friend spoke to me of her burden. Her older son was estranged from her. He had written his mother a terse, shattering letter cutting off all communication. "Don't even send me a Christmas card or a birthday card," he wrote.

"The New Testament has good news in a case like this," I told my friend. "Jesus came to earth for the specific purpose of being our Burden-bearer. He wants to take over 'the government' of our lives (Isaiah 9:6). This isn't any risk for us because He's all love, all good will, all unselfishness. So why don't you simply tell Him that this problem is too much for you, that you want Him to take over the government of your life, including this—and He will."

My friend did just that, relinquished the whole problem to Jesus, the Burden-bearer, including any resentment about her son's attitude and actions.

A year and a half later, the son came to see her. All was forgiven. Today, mother and son, new wife, and baby boy have a great relationship.

I grew up in the Depression. . . . We were down to [living off of] what was in the [church] collection plate each week. However, I was never happier. I had my books and we had each other.

So many families today sacrifice each other. Instead of being with the children, the woman goes off to work so the family can have an extra television set or another car. We have our values all mixed up. And what has it done for this generation of kids? They have more money than any other generation, more records, more motorcycles, more gadgets. And more problems.

—CATHERINE MARSHALL

herever we lived, and for however long, Mother always felt a duty to bring some new natural beauty to our home, something not only for us to enjoy but also to present as sort of house-warming gift to the pastor's family that was to follow us in whichever manse we had once called home. She would, with the enthusiasm of spring itself, plant flowers, shrubs, blossoming bushes and trees and then tenderly care for them.

Well, the years took Mother and Dad to many places, then finally to a not-too-quiet retirement at Evergreen Farm in Virginia. The farm still bristles with projects, and Mother tries to manage all of them—growing the yearly vegetable garden, raising Black Angus cattle, establishing a small nursery of English boxwood, out-smithing Smithfield in curing country hams.

But of all our memorable moments of beauty and bustle at Evergreen, one particular one stands out for me. It was the day Mother first saw Evergreen Farm. She and I were standing on the front porch looking out over the sweep of lawn and shrubbery. Japanese quince and crabapple trees were coming into bloom. Late daffodils punctuated the hillsides.

Mother said to me quietly. "All my married life Dad and I have moved from one manse to another, improving and planting, then moving on, leaving the results of our efforts for the next family.

"Now, at the end of our ministry, it's as if the Lord is saying to us, 'Here it all is with dividends— all you've invested in love and energy— filled up, pressed down and running over. I had it in mind for you all the time.'"

REV. JOHN AND
LEONORA WOOD AT
EVERGREEN FARM

M others all over the world have many praiseworthy traits. But somehow I can't think of a nicer one than that which for so long has characterized my mother—that great, soul-lifting love of nature and eye for beauty that makes her so very blessed, and her daughter so very grateful.

Dear Catherine,

Sunday is Mother's Day and I feel that I am the most fortunate Mother alive. How blessed I am to have three such wonderful, devoted children! And my wonderful grand-children. . . .

I am gradually getting the house in order. Have had a woman cleaning for two days. James is working one day a week in the yard. I'm hoping to find some boys to weed but am shutting my eyes to this need until we can get to them. . . .

Do hope the writing is coming well. Keep me up-to-date, Dearest Love.

Mother

Dear Catherine,

September 27th came before I realized it was so near. As always I had been trying to think of something for your Birthday. But all I could think of was Love . . .Love . . . Love. . . and there surely is no scarcity of that. I am the most fortunate and deeply thankful mother in the world. My "Precious Girlie," that Peter liked to tease me about, means more to me than can ever be expressed. Just a joy that has filled my heart with happiness from her first Birthday, every day. So, a Great Gift of Love is always yours!

Mother

ow can I ever forget some of the memorable family Christmases at our Evergreen Farm in Virginia? . . . The round center table in the kitchen was continuously in use because making things together had become a family tradition. These activities would begin in the summer with making apple butter—so slow in cooking, stir it so constantly—in the huge copper kettle Dad had found at an auction; in making mincemeat; in cracking and shelling nuts and cutting up fruit for fruitcake; and in putting together our special recipe for date-nut roll.

Then after we began spending some summers on Cape Cod, the making and giving of beach-plum jelly also became one of our family traditions. Finding the beach plums in out-of-the-way places in the Cape's sandy soil and gathering them was a family affair. There would follow the pots of cooking plums . . . the night of straining them . . . and finally, dozens of juice glasses all over the kitchen counter filled with the jelly. . . .

At the end of the summer the carefully packed jelly would be carted back to Virginia. Now, near Christmas, we would all be gathered around the big table to wrap the beach-plum jelly, along with strawberry preserves and blackberry jam and apple butter. And in between we would be addressing Christmas cards and making wreaths and garlands of green to twine all the way up the stairs, around every newel post and on every mantel. And on all these activities the blue and white Danish Christmas plates would be looking down from the walls on which they hung—this was their season.

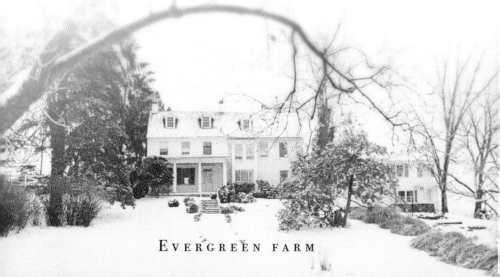

EVERGREEN FARM

n the two years I've been a grandmother, I've learned volumes about living in the Kingdom of God. Mary Elizabeth, [my granddaughter], is able to slip up on my blind side with her teaching. . . . Large, round blue eyes and a piquant nose are framed by blond hair like her mother Edith's. At two, she has sturdy, well-formed legs that carry her into the most unlikely places, and a disarming smile. . . .

What this child does to our household is remarkable. . . . We watch Mary Elizabeth awaken each morning to a world full of wonders. What has become commonplace to us jaded adults still has the freshness of surprise for her. The flying birds, the cloud formations, cows seen in a field, a flower, fragrances, food over which to smack the lips, the rhythm of nursery rhymes and poetry, music–all fill her with excitement. . . .

Through Mary Elizabeth I have been reminded of Christ's extraordinary statement, "Except ye become as little children, ye shall not enter into the kingdom of Heaven." . . . The Kingdom of God! A realm of love and spontaneity and unabashed delight in God and the wondrous world He made. Jesus told us, "Feed my lambs." This means that we are under orders from Him to give our children the best that we know of His love and understanding. But one little girl has made me wonder if, after all, *we* are not the ones who get the feeding.

The obedience
God wants from us
always goes out of love
for Him rather than
out of fear of Him.

—Catherine

s I think back to my own childhood I realize that the moments of purest happiness were fashioned of . . . commonplace ingredients: sitting on my father's lap in his home office (I know now that the feel of his strong arms was nourishment to my spirit), the intensity of wildly competitive Parchesi games, the glorious abandon of coasting down a long hill on my bicycle, the wind in my face, or my enjoyment of a bed of lilies-of-the-valley in our side yard—picking them, burying my nose in their fragrance.

Then there was my early love affair with the rhythm of words. (Memorizing is so easy for a child!) So I took delight in standing on a kitchen chair and reciting "Where Go the Boats?" or "The Swing" from Stevenson's *A Child's Garden of Verse*. My audience of one—my mother or the cook, Josephine—could not have known what pleasure I was getting from listening to and feeling the rhythms tripping off my tongue. . . .

Living in the past or worrying about the future is what spoils the *now* for us adults. Either one keeps us from giving our full attention to the present. . . .

As we go through life, an important factor in learning to live in the present is the realization that each era—from childhood to old age—has its own joyous rewards. I have watched my mother, the inimitable Christy, master this secret and swing gracefully through each successive era. Now 86, she commented recently, "Isn't life fun! I just love all the activity swirling around here."

One particular scene from the moments we have shared often comes back to me. After dinner one evening my mother and I were comfortably settled in our living room. Around us flowed the music of a fine recording, the London Philarmonic Orchestra playing Mendelssohn's *Violin Concerto in E Minor*. As we listened, our hands were busy working on some table mats that were to be a gift. The singing, soaring melody was a delight not just to the eardrums, but to the emotions.

All at once it happened. My heart overflowed with praise. Silently, I lifted all of it to God, aware now of His presence. This quiet room, the comforts and the peace of it. . . .

By Your mercy and grace, Mother is still with us, so gentle, yet so full of her own kind of ginger. You love her, too. Isn't it great that she and I have such rapport that often conversation isn't even necessary. . . . This moment—what delight—what an oasis—in the midst of busy life. . . .

Each such moment that we live is like a rare perfume, the distilled essence of the presentness of life. And the good news is: it is available to every one of us.

ell the years have gone on through two more pastorates and six grandchildren, and time hasn't slowed Mother down much. The home of so-called retirement, Evergreen Farm, now bristles with projects, too, and Mother manages them all. . . .

As I write this, I am thinking wryly of the last three projects Mother thought up last week. She wants to root enough English boxwoods from Evergreen's hundred year old ones to edge all the Eastern seaboard. Then the country hams we cured were so successful, she says she may go into this in a big way, and out-smith Smithfield. And wouldn't I like to look over—in detail—the Quaker "Appalling" at Waterford, Virginia?

Of course, it's obvious that Mother's family adores her—partly because of that exuberant faith that anybody who means business, together with a loving God, can work out any problem, and partly because her zest for living precludes our ever knowing what she'll do next.

Mothers all over the world have many noteworthy traits, but somehow I can't think of a nicer one than that most typical of my mother. . . . The flamboyant plume on that very non-missionary hat she wore on her trip to Asheville as a young girl of nineteen is a sort of symbol of her life. At whatever point she touches life, she always brings a lilt and a lift to it. That's why I smile whenever I think of her.

Come to think of it, I can't imagine any tribute I'd rather have paid to me some day, that that my son would smile in the same way when he thinks of me.

There are all kinds of hands.

There are the pale hands of the song, like lotus buds, soft and white and coldly beautiful.

But as far as I am concerned, there is a greater beauty in my mother's hands as I remember them.

They were warm and soft and red, some of the finger-tips were rough with household care.

—PETER MARSHALL

t age 92, I have lived long past the Biblical span of allotted years. And, as others who share my age know, it has its mixed blessings. I have lived long enough to meet and enjoy eight great-grandchildren, to see the beauty of countless sunsets and green leafings of springs. . . . I have traveled the road of life long enough to know that it is neither smooth or straight, and though I am never really ready for its sudden turns, I am confident about how I should handle them when they come.

In March of 1983, my daughter, Catherine Marshall LeSourd, went into the hospital for some blood tests. I was not prepared for the news telling me that she had died. I was stunned, shattered. I had already lost a husband; my son, Bob; son-in-law Peter Marshall; two little great-grandchildren; and other dear ones. Losing Catherine seemed too much to bear.

But as I sat at the window in my house in Florida weeping and praying, it was as if the Lord came to me. He seemed to be saying: "Don't cry. Catherine is with Me and she is happy."

. . . These are the hardest times, especially when those who are younger than you take their leave, and there are times when I forget and permit myself to think that I am in the midst of death. But this is not so. It is life that surrounds me. Life. Life that is meant to be lived, its riches to be extracted. It is no different now than the day I stood in the snow in Del Rio determined not to give up and go home. No, the Lord's promise is not for those who give up, but for those who forge ahead. . . .

As always, I don't know what the road ahead holds for me. But though my feet aren't steady and my vision is dim, I will walk on down it secure in the promise given me 73 years ago that He *will* hold my right hand and steady me with His assurance:

Fear not; I will help thee.

It's a promise He has always kept.

Leonora Wood,
the indomitable Christy

And so this kind

of friendship

was for life—

yes, and for eternity too.

—CATHERINE MARSHALL
Christy

... thank You. I love her.

Bless her bountifully this day.

Catherine

... years

... shine of y...

"little light...

...ness.

...ther lead you t...

... you always as sweet...

... your proud par...